Dyslexia and me

Expert tips and mindful activities for young people with dyslexia

STUDIO PRESS

A STUDIO PRESS BOOK

First published in the UK in 2020 by Studio Press,
an imprint of Bonnier Books UK,
The Plaza, 535 King's Road, London SW10 0SZ

www.studiopressbooks.co.uk
www.bonnierbooks.co.uk

The typeface used in this book is
Calibri Light size 18pt

1 3 5 7 9 10 8 6 4 2

ISBN 978-1-78741-536-2

Written by Amy Rainbow
Illustrated by Ellie O'Shea
Edited by Frankie Jones
Designed by Rob Ward

A CIP catalogue for this book is available from the British Library
Printed and bound in China

This book belongs to

_____

Welcome to Dyslexia and me!

About this book

This is a book for children and young people with dyslexia. The book is set out in three main sections, as described below. There's lots in the book that you can do on your own, and lots that you can do or share with your grown-ups! Life is easier if you know how to rest and relax, how to really be kind to yourself, and how to be happy with who you are, so some of the pages in this book will help you with that.

All about me

This part of the book is all about you. It helps you to think about who you are, what you like doing, what you're good at and what you want to do in the future. Lots of the book is about you because you're amazing!

Learning with dyslexia

This section looks at what dyslexia is and how it might affect you. It shares tips on ways to learn new things, and helps you to think about how you learn best. Understanding how you learn can make learning much simpler!

Living with dyslexia

This section talks about ways of making life easier. It also gives you tips on taking care of yourself. Self-care (or looking after yourself) is one of the most important life skills you'll ever need, so this part of the book shows you lots of ways to do just that. Sounds good, eh?

The bit for grown-ups

This is the part to show to your grown-ups. It tells them a bit more about dyslexia and what they can do to help you. It also gives them some links to useful websites, but it doesn't give them any fun activities to do, as those are all for you!

Before we begin

This book is not like other books.

In this book you can...

write

draw

colour in

You can also...

go outside

make things, cut things out or stick things in

ask for help

Look out for the pictures above. You will see them at the top of some of the pages in this book to help you know what to do.

You can look at the pages in any order, and some activities can be done again and again.

Who's the expert?

Dyslexia doesn't go away as you grow older, but as you will see in this book, there is a lot you can do to make life easier.

The trick is to try lots of ways of doing things and see what works best for you.

Question

Who is the one person who will always be there to help you?

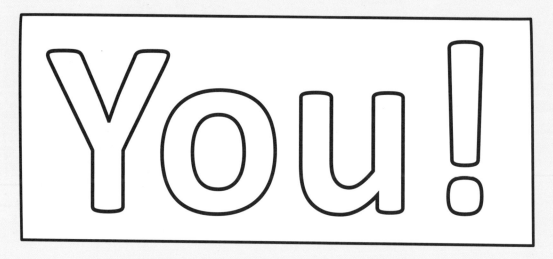

You are the best person to work out what helps you the most.

You are the expert!

Colour in the word 'You!' and say thank you to yourself for always being there!

What a star!

All of the tips and activities in this book have a star near them.

As you try things out, colour in the stars that are next to the ideas you like. Then you know what ideas to use again. You can use these stars to show other people what you like and what they can do to help you too!

Colour in the stars on this page to get warmed up for the first activity!

Are you ready? **Let's go!**

All about me

This is me!

Draw or stick a picture of yourself here.

I live here!

Draw or stick a picture of where you live here.

Happy days

Music

Fill in these shapes with things
that make you happy. You can
add drawings or words or both!

Top tip!   Come back to these pages whenever
you need cheering up!

Top marks!

What are you good at?

Fab friend

Well done!
You are
great at

_____

_____

Top tip!   Ask people for ideas if you get stuck!

Animal magic

What animal would you like to be?

It can be real or imaginary.

Draw your animal here.

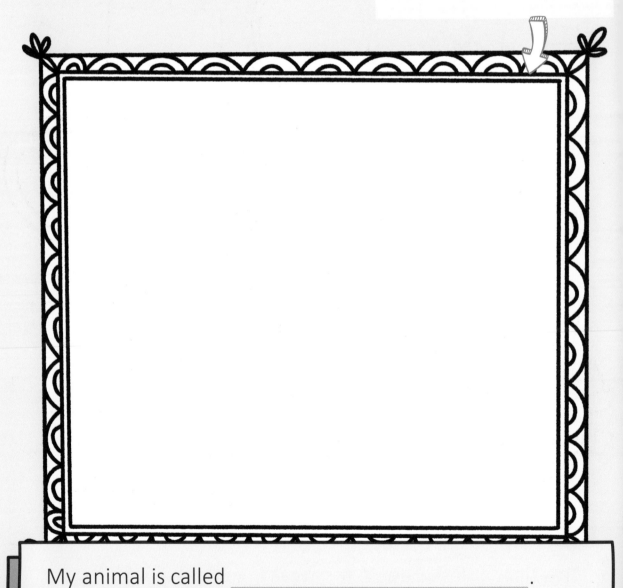

My animal is called _____.

Finish these sentences about your animal.

You can say anything you like!

My animal is

My animal likes

My animal lives

My animal eats

My animal sleeps

My animal wants

I would like to be this animal because

Look how much you've written! Good work!

You're not alone!

There are lots of people in the world.
They are all different! Finish colouring them in.

About 1 in 10 people has dyslexia but you can't see it.

Look carefully at the people below. See if you can find them on the page opposite. When you have found them, put a tick in the box next to them.

Pick three people from this page.
What jobs do you think they do? Write them here.

1. _____

2. _____

3. _____

People with dyslexia can do anything!

Learning with dyslexia

So what is dyslexia?

If you have dyslexia it just means that your brain sometimes works a bit differently from other people's.

It can make some things harder to do, but it can make some things easier! People with dyslexia might find some of these things tricky...

reading

writing

spelling

☐ putting ideas into words

☐ remembering things

☐ telling left from right

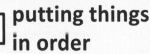

☐ putting things in order

☐ being tidy

☐ being on time

Look at the list again and tick the things you sometimes find tricky.

What helps?

Things can seem harder on some days and easier on others.

It helps if you are...

relaxed

interested

not in a hurry!

Draw or write the answers to the questions in the boxes below.

What helps you to relax?

What are you interested in?

Super skills!

People with dyslexia can be very clever. ☐

They can be practical. ☐

They can be very creative. ☐

They can be great with words. ☐

They can be artistic. ☐

They can have brilliant ideas. ☐

They can be anything they like!

Look at the list again.
Tick the ones which describe you. ☑

Add your own ideas below.

People with dyslexia can be _____ ☐

They can be _____ ☐

They can _____ ☐

Tick the ones which describe you. ☑

Into the future!

Imagine yourself when you are older.

Where would you like to go?

What would you like to do?

I'd like to play the piano.

Draw or write your ideas in the shapes on these two pages.

Inside your mind

This is your brain!

It works very hard...

... even when you are asleep.

Write or draw in the bubbles to show some of the things you dream about.

Your brain works better if you put things in a bit at a time.

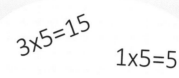

$1x5=5$

$2x5=10$

$3x5=15$

$1x5=5$

$2x5=10$

$4x5=20$

It works even better if you take the time to put things in your brain in different ways.

To learn the five times table you could...

write the sums out

sing a song

study a poster

count marbles

Can you think of other ways to help you learn?

Write or draw your ideas in these boxes.

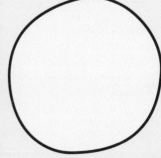

It makes sense!

You can learn by looking, listening, smelling, tasting and feeling. These are our five main senses. Using more than one of them will help you remember things, as the information goes into your memory in different ways.

Connect the words with the right pictures!

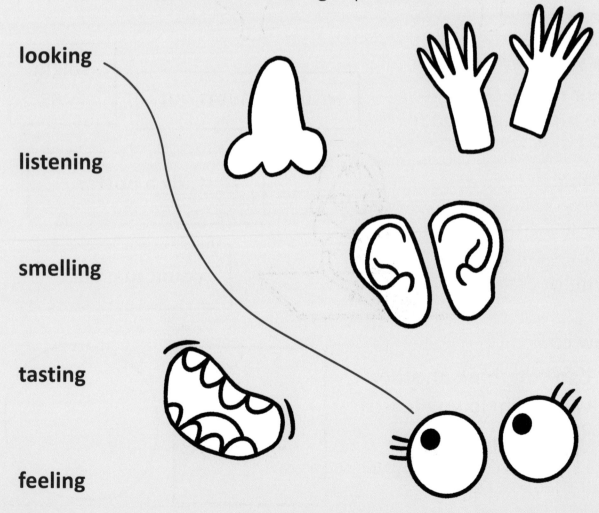

looking

listening

smelling

tasting

feeling

Using all of your senses to learn can also make things more fun!

Here are some ways to learn, using different senses. Use a tick to show which senses are used. ☑

Learning spellings by baking biscuits in the shape of letters.
☐ ☐ ☐ ☐ ☐

Making up a song to help you learn the names of the planets.
☐ ☐ ☐ ☐ ☐

Smelling flowers as you learn their names.
☐ ☐ ☐ ☐ ☐

Listening to a rhyme to help you remember the months of the year.
☐ ☐ ☐ ☐ ☐

Think of something you find tricky to learn. Write or draw it here.

How could you use all your senses to help you learn it? Your ideas can be as silly as you like! Write or draw your ideas here.

Get active!

It can be easier to learn by **doing** a thing.

It would be impossible to learn to swim or ride a bike just by reading about it!

You need someone to help you have a go.

So if you wanted to learn about history, maybe you could act it out.

If you wanted to learn about volcanoes, maybe you could make a model of one.

What activity could you do to help you learn about how plants grow?

Write or draw your idea here.

What activity could you do to help you learn the rules to a new game?

Write or draw your idea here.

Think of something you'd like to learn.

Write or draw your idea here.

What activity could you do to help you learn it?

Write or draw your idea here.

Now try out your ideas...

How did it go?
Tick a face!

Make a note!

If you need to learn spellings, sticking notes to things can help as you will see them every day.

Make a list of 10 things at home with tricky spellings.

1. _____
2. _____
3. _____
4. _____
5. _____

6. _____
7. _____
8. _____
9. _____
10. _____

Ask someone to check your spellings!

Write each word in a box.

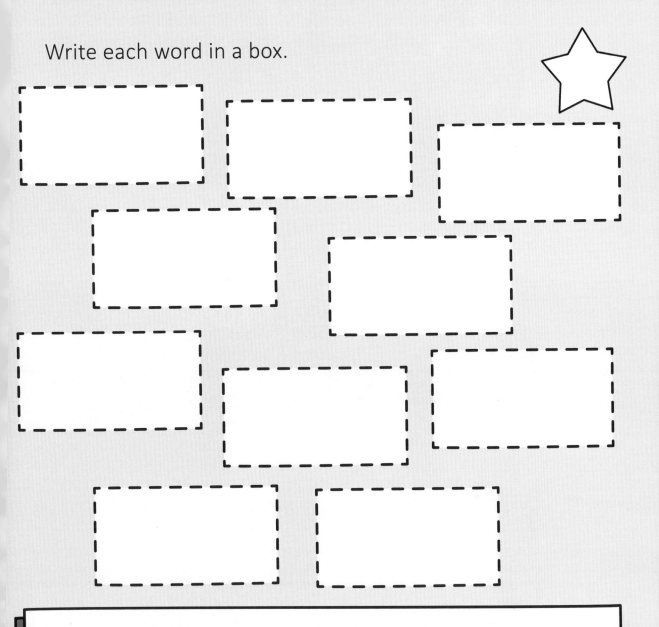

Now cut out the boxes. These will be your sticky notes!

Check with a grown-up, and if it's OK, use tape to stick your notes to the right things at home.

If this works for you, you can make more sticky notes.

This is also a good way to learn words in another language.

Cool colours!

As you colour this in, really look at the shapes of the letters.

Try to use a different colour for each different letter, but if a letter is used more than once, colour it in with the same colour each time.

I am amazing!

You can use colour to help you learn spellings, as it can help you to see patterns in a word.

Lovely letters

You don't always have to write things down on paper. The next few pages give you some ideas about how to use words without writing!

Try them out, and remember to colour in the star next to any ideas you like.

Make words from **magnetic letters.**

we need some
bananas

cup

mum please
buy cat food

slime

woof

You can do this to write messages to people, to learn spellings or just for fun!

Make sentences from **magnetic words.**

You can leave messages for people or make up a story or poem. They might be quite silly if you can't find all the words you want!

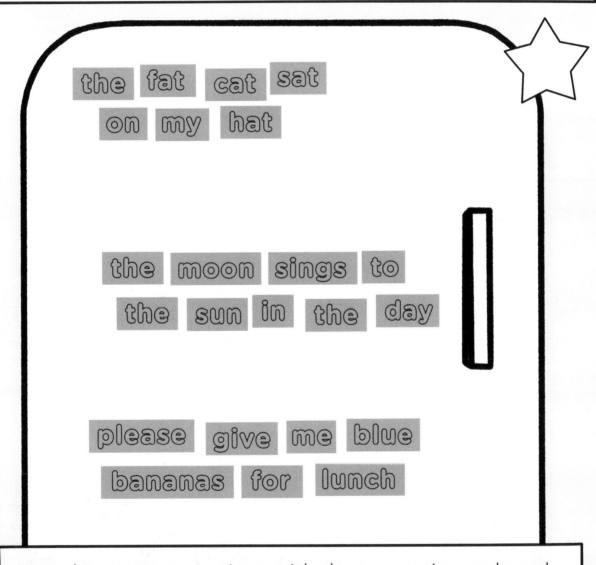

the fat cat sat on my hat

the moon sings to the sun in the day

please give me blue bananas for lunch

Try asking some questions with the magnetic words and see if anyone replies!

Fun with words

There are lots of ways to make words without writing!

Try the ideas in these pictures.

Paint words with water. ☐

Make words in sand. ☐

Make words from things you find at home or outside. ☐ ☆

Tick the ideas off after you've tried them. ☑

On the floor, make four words from things you find in your bedroom.

Draw what you have created in the boxes below.

Reading and typing tips

Words can be easier to read if they are on coloured paper or a coloured screen.

Ask someone to help you try out different colours to see what you prefer.

You can even write or type in colours.

Some people prefer white text on a black screen.

Some people prefer black text on a cream screen.

When you have tried out different screen colours, complete the sentences below.

When I work on a computer, I like the screen colour to be

_____.

I like the colour of the text to be _____.

Letters can be written, typed and printed in lots of different ways. When you use a device like a tablet or laptop, you can change the style of the letters (or font). Each font has its own name. Some fonts are much easier to read.

Below are some different fonts and their names. Tick the ones you find easier to read.

I like this font and find it easy to read. (Arial) ☐

I like this font and find it easy to read. (Times New Roman) ☐

I like this font and find it easy to read. (Esther) ☐

I like this font and find it easy to read. (Verdana) ☐

I like this font and find it easy to read. (Tahoma) ☐

I like this font and find it easy to read. (Comic Sans) ☐

I like this font and find it easy to read. (OpenDyslexic) ☐

Give me space!

Words can be easier to read if they are bigger and more spaced out. The sentences below are all in the same font, but the font size is different.

Tick the ones you find easier to read. ✓

This text is very big.

This text is very small.

This text is medium sized.

The main font used in this book is 18pt.

You can change the amount of space between lines too. Some people with dyslexia miss out lines of text when they are reading, so adding space between the lines can help.

You can change the amount of space between lines too. Some people with dyslexia miss out lines of text when they are reading, so adding space between the lines can help.

Was one of the paragraphs above easier to read? If so, tick the one you prefer. ✓

Ask someone to help you try out different fonts, font sizes, line spacing and screen colour on a computer to see what you prefer.

 Type a few sentences about yourself using the font, font size and line spacing you prefer. Print your work out and stick it here!

Reading for meaning

Do you sometimes read a whole page then have no idea what it said? This can be common for people with dyslexia as they are working so hard to read each word that their brain finds it tricky to take in all of the meaning too.

Here are some things you can do to help...

Read the page twice. ☐

Highlight important words.* ☐

Underline important words.* ☐

Write down important points as you read. ☐

Write down some questions before you read so that you know what information you're looking for. ☐

Use text to speech software to read the page out to you. Then you can focus on the meaning rather than reading each word. ☐

Use audio books and read along at the same time. ☐

Over the next few days, try at least five of these and tick the ones you have tried.

*Remember to only do this in books that belong to you!

Get it out!

People with dyslexia often have very good ideas and imaginations.

Sometimes they find it hard to put these ideas into words or onto paper.

Over the next few days, try out some of these ideas and tick them off when you've tried them. Remember to colour in the stars next to the ones you like.

Instead of writing something you could...

☐ ☆ Draw it – a story can be drawn as a comic strip

☐ ☆ Act it out

☐ ☆ Make it

☐ ☆ Sing it

☐ ☆ Paint it

☐ ☆ Say it

☐ ☆ Record your ideas using a phone or voice recorder

☐ ☆ Film yourself explaining your ideas

All of these can be used to show people how you're feeling too.

You could also get someone to ask you questions or even ask yourself questions. When writing a story, if you don't know where to start, you could ask yourself who was there, what they did, how they felt and so on. Very soon you'll have the start of your story.

You could also try speech to text software. This is amazing as it types up your ideas as you say them!

Mind maps

Sometimes your ideas might come out in a funny order. Making a mind map is a great way to see how these ideas fit together. A mind map is a bit like a tree with colourful branches and twigs!

You can create mind maps with computer software, or scribble them on paper. Mind maps can be used for lots of things, like planning a story or packing for your holiday.

You can use pictures instead of words if you prefer.

You can use the mind map
as it is, or turn it into a list.

Things to take on holiday		Packed?
clothes	socks	✓✓
	pants	✓
	shoes	✓
	shorts	
beach	towel	
	book	
	kite	
	swimming costume	
car journey	snacks	
caravan	torch	

Look back at the mind map and
fill in the items that are missing
from the list.

More mind maps!

Make your own mind map of things you like to do.

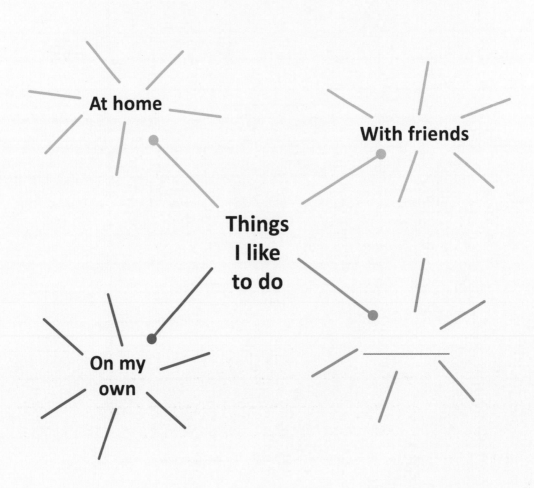

At home

With friends

Things I like to do

On my own

Add more branches and twigs if you like!

Have a go at filling in the mind map below to plan a story.

You don't need to know everything about your story yet, as making the mind map helps give you ideas!

Add in the people in your story and the places they go to. You can change the headings if you like, but a good story often has problems to be overcome, so this mind map has branches for problems and solutions.

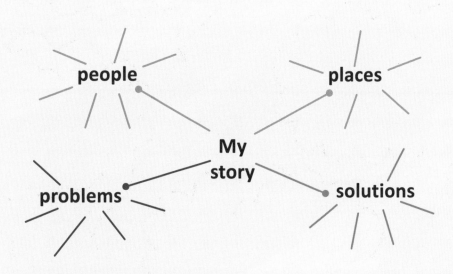

people

places

My story

problems

solutions

Now use your mind map to make up a whole story. You could tell the story to someone, write it down or record it for yourself.

Mind maps can be used for anything where you need to get your ideas out. Once they are in your mind map you can think about what order they can go in.

Top tip!

Some mind maps or lists can be used again and again, so make sure you make copies of them or save them on a computer.

Brilliant brains

This part of the book has shown you some ways to learn and remember things.

How do you think **you** learn best?

By using lots of senses?

By using mind maps?

By making lists?

By making up songs?

Fill in these brains with your ideas!

Living with Dyslexia

One of a kind!

Having dyslexia isn't all about reading and writing. It sometimes means you forget or lose things easily, or get muddled about what to do next. This can be very frustrating for someone with dyslexia, especially when they are doing their best and other people don't realise!

The great thing about people is that they are all different. You're one of a kind!

The good news is that if you know what you find tricky, you can find ways of making those things easier. This part of the book gives you ideas to try, and has lots of tips about looking after yourself. This is super important for someone with dyslexia because they often have to work harder than other people just to keep up.

Colour in the butterflies on this page. They are all different! They are all beautiful!

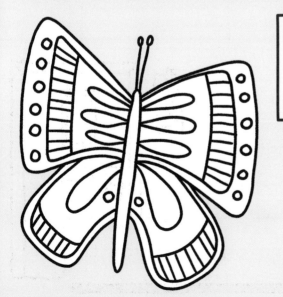

Don't forget!

Do you sometimes forget to take things with you? It can help to make a list and tick things off as you pack them.

Things to pack in my school bag	Monday	Tuesday	Wednesday	Thursday	Friday	
Lunch						
Pencil case						
Reading book						
Water						
P.E. Kit						
Spelling book						

If you make a list on card or paper, you can photocopy it and use it again and again. If you make one on a computer, you can save it and print one off weekly.

Top tip!   Stick the list up where you can't miss it.

Fill in the list on this page with things you need to take with you every day. Use the list on the opposite page for ideas. Use lots of colour and pictures too.

Things to pack in my school bag	Monday	Tuesday	Wednesday	Thursday	Friday	

When you have finished, cut it out, ask someone to photocopy it, and stick it up where you will see it every day.

This page is blank!

Sing it!

Do you sometimes forget things?
Try making up a song to help.

Clean my teeth, brush my hair,
pack my bag and go downstairs...

You can even add dance moves or act out the things you need to remember!

Remember, remember...

Use your imagination and add lots of sounds and smells and colours.

If you have a list of things you need to remember, it can help to put them into a story.

Imagine you're going to a friend's birthday party and you need to take a **card**, a **present**, your **boots** and a **coat**.

Making your story silly or funny can help it to stick in your memory.

How will you remember everything? Try making up a story with them all in...

Playing the film of this story in your mind will help you remember all the things to take.

| You are at home when a giant birthday card lands outside with a bang! | You run out to see that it has squashed the present. | A pair of yellow boots start jumping on the card | It's so noisy that you throw your coat over it to make it quiet. |

Make up your own silly story to help you remember these things – a **cup**, a **dog**, a **banana** and some **sunglasses**.

Really try to see and hear it all in your mind.

You can even add touch, taste and smell.

Draw your story here.

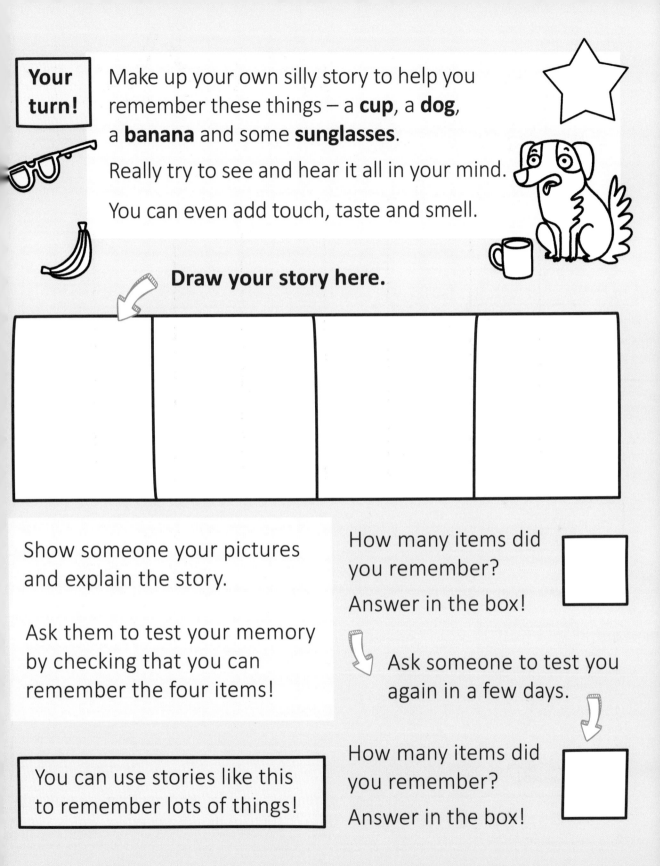

Show someone your pictures and explain the story.

Ask them to test your memory by checking that you can remember the four items!

You can use stories like this to remember lots of things!

How many items did you remember?

Answer in the box!

Ask someone to test you again in a few days.

How many items did you remember?

Answer in the box!

Timetable time!

Timetables can help you be in the right place at the right time.

	Lesson 1	Lesson 2	Break	Lesson 3	Lunch	Lesson 4	Lesson 5
Monday	Maths	P.E.		English		Drama	Art
Tuesday	Cooking	English		Maths		French	Music
Wednesday	I.C.T.	Maths		French		P.E.	P.E.
Thursday	Forest School	Forest School		History		English	Science
Friday	English	Dance		Science		Art	Maths

Quick quiz... Answer these questions in the boxes!

1. What colour are the P.E. lessons?

2. How many English lessons are there in a week?

3. What is the last lesson on a Monday?

4. What day is cooking on?

5. How many days is maths on?

Ask someone to check your answers if you like.

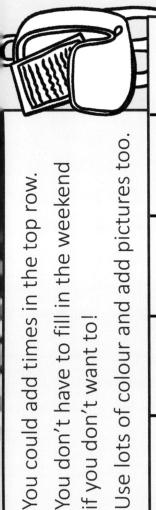

Your turn!

Fill in this timetable with your lessons or things you do every day.

You could add times in the top row.

You don't have to fill in the weekend if you don't want to!

Use lots of colour and add pictures too.

Monday							
Tuesday							
Wednesday							
Thursday							
Friday							
Saturday							
Sunday							

When you've finished, cut it out carefully.

Ask someone to photocopy it so you can keep a copy in more than one place.

Time for kindness!

Doing kind things for others can make them happy and make you happy too! It can be as simple as smiling or saying something nice.

In the chart below, write the names of five people you would like to be kind to. Then write down what you plan to do.

Tick things off as you do them.

Did it work?

Name	Plan	Done ☑	Did it work?
Anusha	Eat lunch together	☑	Yes, and it was fun!
Freddie	Watch movie together	☐	
		☐	
		☐	
		☐	
		☐	

Top tip! You don't need a chart to be kind to people every day. Try to do kind things whenever you can and add more happiness to the world.

Chop it up!

Sometimes it's hard to start a task as it seems too big!

Tidy your room!

Breaking tasks into small chunks can help. You can then do one chunk at a time and tick them off until the job is done.

	Tidy my room				
1	Put rubbish in the bin		✓	✓	
2	Put clothes away		✓	✓	
3	Tidy my books		✓	✓	
4	Make my bed		✓	✓	
5	Put my games away		✓		
6	Relax		✓		

Your turn! Think of a big task that you often do – maybe tidying your room, getting ready in the mornings or getting ready for bed.

Write the task here.

1			☐ ☐ ☐ ☐ ☐
2			☐ ☐ ☐ ☐ ☐
3			☐ ☐ ☐ ☐ ☐
4			☐ ☐ ☐ ☐ ☐
5			☐ ☐ ☐ ☐ ☐
6			☐ ☐ ☐ ☐ ☐
7			☐ ☐ ☐ ☐ ☐
8			☐ ☐ ☐ ☐ ☐

Now break the task into small chunks, and write and draw them here.

Cut this table out and stick it up at home. You can use it five times, ticking off each chunk of the task as you do it.

Top tip! Make tables like this for all your big tasks. Photocopy them to use again and again, or create them on a computer and print lots of copies.

Another blank page!

Find the words!

q	v	g	s	p	s	t	r	o	n	g	c
z	e	s	i	n	g	p	f	t	v	b	m
y	f	h	f	a	p	k	i	n	d	v	s
x	h	a	p	p	y	d	s	b	t	e	n
g	u	d	s	a	z	r	e	a	v	b	t
p	o	i	y	f	u	n	m	n	x	c	n
f	d	g	b	v	c	t	b	s	u	n	v
s	d	f	a	s	m	i	l	e	c	s	b
f	l	o	w	e	r	r	a	q	h	n	z
x	s	d	v	r	g	h	j	i	r	o	p
d	t	c	o	o	l	y	m	c	e	z	u
p	s	s	r	z	m	c	g	r	e	s	t

Words to find: fun ✓ happy ✓ cool ✓ smile

kind ✓ (strong) sun ✓

rest ✓ flower ✓ sing ✓

Look after yourself!

It is important to eat and drink well.

Draw some of your favourite healthy meals, snacks and drinks here

Eating and drinking well will help you to...

... keep active!

Draw or write in the boxes to show how you like to stay active.

Staying active is good for your body and mind. It will help you to...

... rest well!

Draw or write in the boxes to show how you like to relax.

Eating and drinking well and staying active also help you to...

... sleep well!

Draw your
bed here.

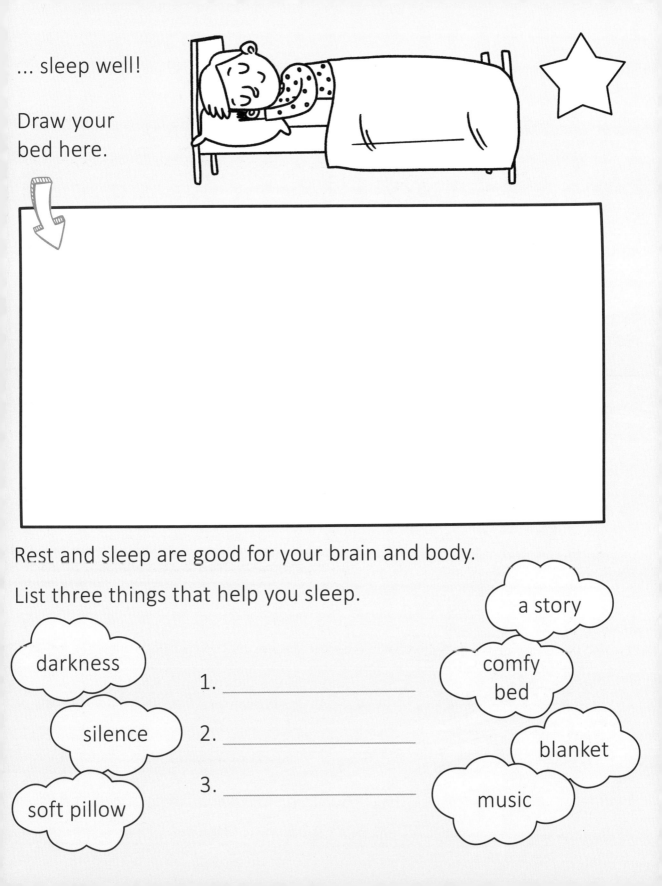

Rest and sleep are good for your brain and body.

List three things that help you sleep.

darkness

silence

soft pillow

1. _____

2. _____

3. _____

a story

comfy
bed

blanket

music

My calm place

Draw and colour a calm place to relax in.

Lie down and close your eyes.

Go to your calm place in your mind, and stay there for a few minutes.

Which word best describes how you feel in your calm place?

Top tip!
You can go to your calm place in your mind whenever you need to relax.

My fun place

Draw and colour a fun place to explore.

Lie down and close your eyes.

In your mind, go on an adventure in your fun place.

Which word best describes how you feel in your fun place?

Top tip!
You can go to your fun place in your mind whenever you want an adventure or need cheering up!

Keep moving!

As well as keeping you fit and strong, exercising in the morning can give you lots of energy for the day ahead. Exercising in the evening can tire you out and help you sleep!

Try the exercises in the pictures at different times of day to see how they make you feel.

20 star jumps

10 second plank

Dance to a lively song!

15 squats

20 side stretches

Cut out the chart and stick it up at home!

Do at least three of these every day for a week.

Fill in the chart as you go. ☑

	20 star jumps	10 second plank	Dance to a lively song	15 squats	20 side stretches
Monday	☐	☐	☐	☐	☐
Tuesday	☐	☐	☐	☐	☐
Wednesday	☐	☐	☐	☐	☐
Thursday	☐	☐	☐	☐	☐
Friday	☐	☐	☐	☐	☐
Saturday	☐	☐	☐	☐	☐
Sunday	☐	☐	☐	☐	☐

Room for improvement!

Can you think of three things you'd like to be better at?

Write them in the blue boxes below.

Now think about how you could get better at those things.

Write your ideas in the red boxes. Like this.

I would like to be better at **swimming.**	I shall go to the pool every Sunday.	I shall learn how to tread water.
I would like to be better at	I shall	I shall
I would like to be better at	I shall	I shall
I would like to be better at	I shall	I shall

Top tip! You can set targets for anything you want to be better at.

Kind words

When someone says something kind to you, write it in one of these shapes.

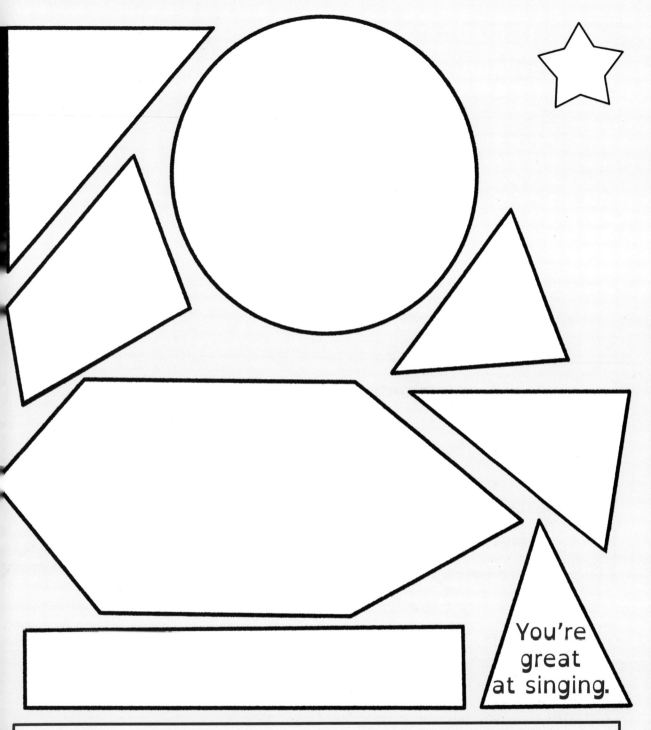

You're great at singing.

Top tip! Come back to these pages whenever someone says something kind or whenever you need reminding of how great you are!

Help!

It's good to tell someone what you need.

Then they can help. What do you need?

Fill in the blanks below.

Sometimes I feel _sad_
so I need _a hug_ .

Sometimes I _work slowly_
so I need _more time_ .

Sometimes I don't understand instructions so I need
_____ .

Sometimes I forget things so I need _____
_____ .

Sometimes I feel frustrated so I need _____
_____ .

Sometimes I don't understand the question so I need _____ .

Sometimes I find things hard so I need _____ .

Sometimes I want to _____
so I need _____ .

Sometimes I am _____
so I need _____ .

Sometimes I _____
so I need _____ .

Sometimes I _____
so I need _____ .

Top tip!   Ask for help! We all need help sometimes.

Who can help?

Lots of people will be happy to help you wit all sorts of things.

Grandad

Helps with maths

Fill in these picture frames to show who you can ask for help.

You could draw the person or stick in a photo.

Make a jar of joy!

Find an empty jar and decorate it how you like!

Find 10 bits of paper.

Jar of joy

On each one, write or draw something that makes you happy.

Fold them up and put them into your jar.

Whenever you want to feel happy, pull a bit of paper from your jar of joy and do what it says!

Top tip! You can add ideas to your jar of joy any time.

Calm clouds

Sometimes it can be good for your body
and mind to do almost nothing at all!

Watch the clouds!

Blow them along!

What shapes can you see?

Imagine you are a cloud!

Top tip! If you want to feel calm, even if you can't go outside, close your eyes and imagine you're a cloud floating through the summer sky...

Make a cup of kindness!

Find a big cup or bowl.

Cup of
kindness

Give three small pieces of paper to 10 different friends or people in your family.

Ask them to write a kind thing about you on each piece of paper and then fold them up.

Don't read them!

Put them into your cup.

Your jokes are very silly.

Pull one piece of paper out every morning and read it. This should make you smile every day for a month!

Top tip! You could put the pieces of paper back into the cup and use them again, or you could ask people to write different things and start again.

Yoga time!

See if you can hold each yoga pose for 10 seconds.

Turtle pose

Cat pose

Shark pose

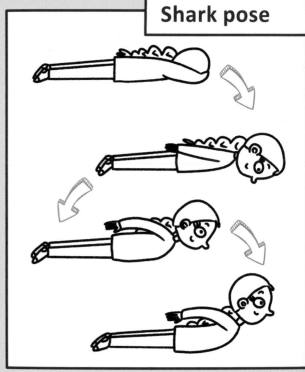

You could do this every bedtime to help you relax.

Bird pose

Tree pose

Frog pose

Do each pose every day for a week and colour in a smiley face each time.

Take care!

This book has shown you some ways to take care of yourself.

How are you going to take care of yourself?

By eating well?

By getting more exercise?

By relaxing more?

By asking for help?

Fill in these hearts with your ideas!

Top tip!   Come back to this page whenever you need more self-care!

Colour these in and read them out loud as often as you like!

I am wonderful!

I am brilliant!

Be happy!

I am great!

Yes I can!

Life is an adventure!

Go for it!

Smile!

Happy day!

I can do it!

Today is a good day!

Think big!

Top tip! Tell yourself positive things like this every day as it can help improve your mood, even if you don't believe them at first!

The bit for grown-ups

Living with dyslexia can be exhausting. Most people associate dyslexia with struggling to read and write, but are often unaware of the many other possible problems that dyslexic people face.

Having dyslexia means that your brain processes information slightly differently from usual, which is what can cause issues with spelling, writing, reading and breaking words down into different sounds. Reading a word does not easily become automatic for the dyslexic learner, so they may sound out the word 'cat' on one line and have to go through the same process again a few lines later. In addition, what may seem like simple tasks, such as copying out a word, can be difficult, and the dyslexic child is often very aware that they are working more slowly than others, which adds to their distress and in turn negatively affects performance.

They may have trouble with sequencing (for example, remembering the order of days of the week), memory, remembering left and right, organisation, and can struggle to process verbal instructions or seem not to be concentrating.

They might have trouble learning to tell the time or even have trouble grasping how much time has passed or how long things take, which can make them late for things.

Dyslexia is in no way linked to intelligence, so a dyslexic child is often disappointed with their own work when they know they haven't produced something that truly shows their ability. They can work twice as hard and have half as much as others to show for it, so imagine their frustration if the adults around them then suggest that they haven't tried very hard! For some learners, low self-esteem and lack of confidence affect them early on, and it is easy to see why some people with dyslexia find it easier to avoid academic learning as much as possible.

However, there are many positives to dyslexia too, and with a sound understanding of their own strengths and weaknesses, every person with dyslexia can put together a toolkit of coping strategies to help them navigate tricky areas of life and learning, and build on their skills and strong points to thrive. People with dyslexia are often creative, great at problem solving and seeing things differently, imaginative and good with spatial awareness. They can go into any profession they choose as long as they realise that dyslexia needn't hold them back.

So what can you do to help? Do some research to find out more about dyslexia, then try to find out how it affects the specific child you're supporting. Go through this book with them, and discuss what works best and what strategies they can use in different situations. Repetition or over-learning are important, and multi-sensory learning helps the child retain information. Be generous and genuine with your praise, and if you are frustrated with them, know that they are even more frustrated with themselves. If something

isn't working, put it aside and try it another time in a different way. Let the child read anything they enjoy, even if there are lots of pictures and not many words. They are building their confidence and their pleasure of reading. Encourage the child to add notes in books or to underline or highlight key points or new words, however strange that might feel! Make learning as fun as possible and focus on what's important. If learning a list of spellings is making a child miserable then do it a different way, and make sure that they know there are plenty of people who are successful and happy but can't spell!

Many of the exercises in this book are to help boost self-esteem, as dyslexia can have a big effect on a person's image of themselves. If a child learns by being outside and observing nature then use that and follow their interests. An unmotivated and tired child won't learn, but an eager and energetic one will.

Schools should be able to offer advice and support but you may need to make sure they are aware of how your child likes to learn, and if there has so far been no official diagnosis of dyslexia it's worth ensuring that this happens, so that the child's needs are properly assessed. There are simple things which can make a huge difference, such as altering font size and spacing, changing the colour of paper used or the computer screen background, making sure that there is no glare on a page or on the whiteboard, or using a reading ruler or coloured overlay. Visual stress can sometimes go hand in hand with dyslexia, so an assessment with a behavioural optometrist is a good idea.

There are plenty of apps and assistive software, so it's worth looking at what's available. Text to speech and speech to text software can be invaluable, as well as software which helps with spelling and mind mapping. If writing is always a real struggle, perhaps a computer could be used instead. During exam time the school may allow the child to use a computer and give them extra time but this needs planning in advance. This is also true in higher education, where assistive software for dyslexic students is the norm and most assignments are done on computer. We need to focus on bringing up happy, healthy children who are able to fulfil their potential, and that may mean that we need to reassess our own ideas of what's important in regards to essential skills and abilities, so that we can fully celebrate a child's own unique abilities and successes.

Hopefully this activity book has given you some useful ideas on how to best support a child with dyslexia. For further information, here are just a few of the many organisations who can offer information and advice.

British Dyslexia Association
www.bdadyslexia.org.uk

The Dyslexia-SpLD Trust
www.thedyslexia-spldtrust.org.uk

BABO:
The British Association of Behavioural Optometrists
www.babo.co.uk